BIG BEND OUTDOORS

A detailed guide to canoeing, camping, hiking, biking and more in Florida's Big Bend region.

by Richard and Claudia Farren

On the cover:

Front: Cape St. George Island State Preserve
    Pinhook River
    Slave Canal

Back: Tallahassee-St. Marks Historic Railroad State Trail
    Wacissa River

ISBN 0-9632059-2-7

Library of Congress Catalog Card Number 94-60748

Published by
Woodland Productions
2208 Hickory Court
Tallahassee, FL 32311.

First Edition

Printed in the United States by
Artcraft Printers
Tallahassee, FL

INTRODUCTION

Stress Relief

The outdoors used to be the place we went to chase and harvest food, because that's what we were, hunters and gatherers. Today we need the outdoors for an additional important reason — as the cure for the disease of the modern world, stress.

There's no doubt that time spent in the outdoors can reinvigorate the most depressed spirit. It doesn't have to be a full-blown outing, or a fifty-mile hike; a couple hours spent on a near-by trail, or just a drive through a park or wildlife refuge can make all the difference in how we feel about ourselves and the world around us.

The Big Bend area is blessed with an incredible variety of these outdoor opportunities. Crystal-clear, spring-fed rivers, scenic hiking trails, wildlife refuges, state parks, and even a national forest are readily available for our use.

We encourage you to take advantage of these opportunities. We feel it will enrich your life as it has ours.

We also encourage you to always be safe in the outdoors. Take the necessary precautions against heat, cold, rain and mosquitos. When feasible, take along a compass, first aid kit, and any published maps available for your chosen activity.

Also, take advantage of people knowledgeable of your activity or destination. In the back of this book is a listing of organizations that regularly sponsor trips into the outdoors. Make contact — without exception they have much to offer both the experienced and beginning outdoor enthusiast.

Rick and Claudia Farren

Table Of Contents

Hiking 7

Florida National Scenic Trail 9

Aucilla Sinks Trail 13

Bradwell Bay 17

Leon Sinks 21

Canoeing 25

Aucilla River 27

St. Marks River 30

Wacissa River 33

The Slave Canal 38

Wakulla River 41

Biking 45

Tallahassee-St. Marks Historic Railroad State

Trail 47

Munson Hills Off-Road Bicycle Trail 50

Biking the Dikes of the St. Marks Refuge 53

Table Of Contents

State Parks 57

Florida Caverns State Park 59

St. Joe State Park 63

St. George Island State Park 67

Cape St. George Island State Preserve 71

Torreya State Park 75

Apalachicola National Forest . . . 79

St. Marks National Wildlife Refuge 85

Information Resources 90

Hikers on a trail that leads to the old site of the town of Port Leon.

Hiking

Hiking opportunities abound in the Big Bend area. You can choose from a quarter mile nature trail, a 100-mile wilderness experience, or just about anything in-between.

In general, hiking conditions in this part of Florida present few serious challenges. Most of the trails are level and dry, however, during rainy periods, some of the trails in the coastal floodplain can have standing water.

Fall, winter and spring are the best hiking seasons because of the mild temperatures. Hiking in the summer requires precautions against dehydration and insects. In addition to mosquitoes; ticks, yellow flies, horse flies and wasps can be out in abundance in the warmer months. Near the Gulf coast, sand gnats (no-see-ums) can turn a pleasant trip into a miserable outing.

Not one of these things are sufficient reason not to enjoy the outdoors year-round in North Florida. With the right precautions, (drinking water, insect repellant, sunscreen, snakebite kit, compass and a map) hiking in the Big Bend can open the outdoors to places rich in wildlife and scenery enjoyed by only a few. And in some cases the hiker will even glimpse lands largely unchanged since the arrival of man to this land over 10,000 years ago.

For hiking and backpacking opportunities in addition to those covered in this section, see chapters on Torreya State Park, Wakulla Springs State Park, St. Marks National Wildlife Refuge, and Apalachicola National Forest.

A wooden bridge on the Florida National Scenic Trail presents hikers with a picturesque view of the Pinhook River.

Florida National Scenic Trail
Refresh your soul with a walk through the wilderness

Created as an idea by an act of Congress in 1983, the Florida National Scenic Trail, one of eight such trails across the country, is gradually becoming a reality. Sometime early in the next century, the 1300-mile footpath will connect Gulf Islands National Seashore near Pensacola, to the Everglades.

In the Big Bend area a well-established, 110-mile section crosses the St. Marks National Wildlife Refuge and the Apalachicola National Forest. In 1988, this became the first section of the original Florida Trail to be dedicated as a Florida National Scenic Trail. To be part of the National Scenic Trail System a trail has to provide certain scenic and recreational values.

A hiker walking through all or part of these two large areas of federal land will be treated to an incredible sampling of vistas and habitats. The trail winds through live oak and cabbage palm hammocks, mature pine forests, and wet, dark swamps. It looks out over sink holes and salt marsh vistas. It passes through a 19th century ghost town, a long-abandoned turpentine gathering camp, confederate salt-works, and the site of a moonshine operation. It follows twisting wilderness rivers, crosses sandy-bottomed creeks, and sneaks past hidden, tree-shrouded lakes.

Those are the big sights, but there are also the thousands of small sights—venus flytraps, pitcher plants, golden orb spiders, wild grapes, wild hibiscus flowers, warblers and woodpeckers.

St. Marks National Wildlife Refuge
The Florida Trail enters the St. Marks Refuge off Highway 98, three-quarters of a mile west of the bridge over the Aucilla River. Forty-three miles later it exits the refuge on U.S. Highway 319, 1.1 miles west of Medart. A short section of the trail follows the St. Marks Historic Railroad

9

Bicycle Trail and Highway 98 between unconnected sections of the refuge.

While in the refuge it leads the hiker through cypress swamps, old growth forests, longleaf pine forests, and past wide-open expanses of a salt marsh with its "wheat-field" look of spartina and needlerush grasses. It also follows miles of dikes rimming watery impoundments that support a variety of wildlife from alligators to wading birds.

At one point the trail crosses through the old town site of Port Leon, a shipping port on the St. Marks River about a mile below the current town of St. Marks. Port Leon was only inhabited for 12 years before a hurricane blasted it out of existence in 1843. The town was re-established at the current site of Newport.

A mile north of the Port Leon site the trail crosses the St. Marks River into the town of St. Marks. You'll have to hail a friendly boater for a ride across the river. From there the trail continues through two more sections of the refuge that are largely characterized by pine forests and hardwoods. For more information see the chapter on the St. Marks National Wildlife Refuge on page 85.

Apalachicola National Forest

The trail enters the Apalachicola National Forest at the point that it leaves the refuge, (1.1 miles west of Medart) and exits the forest 67 miles later on State Road 379 at the northwest corner of the national forest boundary.

In the forest the Florida Trail leads to hidden sink holes, park-like longleaf forests; and dark, dank swamps. Because of the many unpaved roads through the forest, it's relatively easy to access various sections of the trail for one-day hikes.

For more information on this section of the trail see the chapters on Bradwell Bay, Leon Sinks, the Apalachicola National Forest and the St. Marks National Wildlife Refuge.

Trail Markings

The Florida Trail is marked with orange blazes on tree trunks about six feet off the ground. A double blaze signifies a sharp turn in the trail. Side trails are marked with blue blazes. Florida Trail signs (see page 11) often mark places where the trail crosses a major road.

Camping

Camping is permitted in the St. Marks Refuge only at designated campsites along the trail. A permit must be obtained a full 15 days prior to your trip. Camping is permitted about anywhere in the national forest, plus there are a number of developed recreation areas available. There are some camping restrictions during hunting season, a time when it's also a good idea to wear bright-colored clothing.

Incidentally, the Florida Trail is maintained strictly by volunteers. If you feel the urge, you might consider volunteering for one of the dozens of trail maintenance hikes held every spring.

For more information on the Florida National Scenic Trail contact the Florida Trail Association, P.O. Box, 13708, Gainesville, FL 32604-1708; 1(800) 343-1882 or 1(904) 378-8823.

For a map of the trail through the St. Marks National Wildlife Refuge and additional information contact: St. Marks National Wildlife Refuge, P.O. Box 68, St. Marks, FL, 32355; 1(904) 925-6121.

For information and a map of the Apalachicola National Forest which shows the trail and developed camp sites send $2.00 to the U.S. Forest Service, 325 John Knox Road, Suite F-100, Tallahassee, FL. 32303.

Florida Trail signs often mark places where the trail crosses a road or highway. The trail itself is marked with orange blazes on tree trunks.

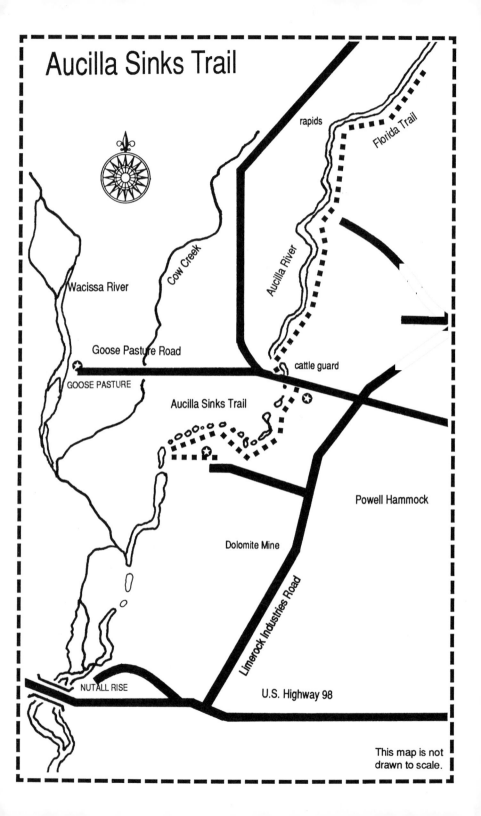

Aucilla Sinks Trail

A wonderland of sinks and forest awaits the hiker on this unique trail

Ten miles from the Gulf of Mexico, in eastern Jefferson County, the Aucilla River is captured by a sink hole. For the next few miles the river's waters can be seen in a series of about 20 sink holes. The river returns to the surface five miles from the Gulf near the small community of Nutall Rise.

A 4.2-mile section of the Florida Trail passes by 16 of these sink holes affording a wonderful, scenic hiking experience.

The sinks come in a variety of sizes and adornments. Many are surrounded by exposed limestone that has been carved and shaped by flowing water; some are open and sunny with a carpeting of aquatic vegetation; still others are dark and mysterious, hidden beneath a canopy of towering hardwoods. There's even a visible current in one or two of the larger sinks.

It may seem obvious that the sink holes were created by the underground river, which flows across the surface from sink to sink during flooded conditions. Actually, the river had very little to do with the original formation of the sinks and is simply following the same fault line that the sinks have formed along.

Like sink holes all over Florida, they were created by rainfall that became slightly acidic after percolating through the organic soil. The water ate away at the limestone as it worked its way down to the aquifer, slowly forming a system of caverns. When a cavern collapses it forms a sink hole. Sometime in the past a sink hole caved in close enough to the Aucilla to capture the river and direct it into the cavern system below.

The maintained trail passes through a mixed hardwood forest, and occasionally through upland sections of pine and palmetto. Some of the more common trees along the trail are oak, ash, magnolia, holly, dogwood, hawthorn, ironwood, sable palm and pine.

Every sinkhole is different, from the dark and mysterious, to the open and sunny.

A variety of birds can often be seen along the trail including owls, woodpeckers, warblers, and vireos.

Difficulty

The terrain is mostly level with a few small rises. During periods of heavy rainfall sections of the trail can be wet or even flooded. Because of the trail's location near the edges of sink holes it can be dangerous when flooded. During the warmer months the woods are loaded with mosquitoes, no-see-ums and chiggers. Always carry water, a compass and insect repellant. Also watch for poison ivy in the wetter areas.

Sink holes are delicate and susceptible to damage from careless visitors. It's best to stay away from the edge and avoid the temptation to climb down to the water. When vegetation is destroyed or a new path created to the water it can cause an increase in erosion.

Directions

The Aucilla Sinks Trail is located near the border of Jefferson and Taylor County off Highway 98. To reach the southern end of the trail turn north on Limerock Industries Road, the second paved road east of the Highway 98 bridge over the Aucilla River. The turn is a little over 16 miles east of Newport.

The pavement ends just past the Limerock Industries quarry. Go 2.8 miles from Highway 98 to the first dirt road past the quarry and turn left. The southern end of the Sinks Trail starts on the right, about one mile down this road. A double orange blaze on a small tree marks the spot.

To find the northern end of the trail, return to Limerock Industries Road, turn left and go 1.5 miles to an intersection of two dirt roads. Turn left again and go a little over one mile to a cattle guard in the road. This is where the Florida Trail crosses the road.

As part of the Florida Trail, the Aucilla Sinks Trail is marked by orange blazes painted on tree trunks a few feet above the ground. A single blaze means the trail continues in the same general direction. A double blaze means you should look for a sharp turn. It's a good idea to always have the next blaze in sight to avoid losing the trail.

For more information on the Aucilla Sinks and other sections of the Florida Trail contact the Florida Trail Association, P.O. Box 13708, Gainesville, FL 32604 - 1708; (904) 378-8823 or 1-800-343-1882.

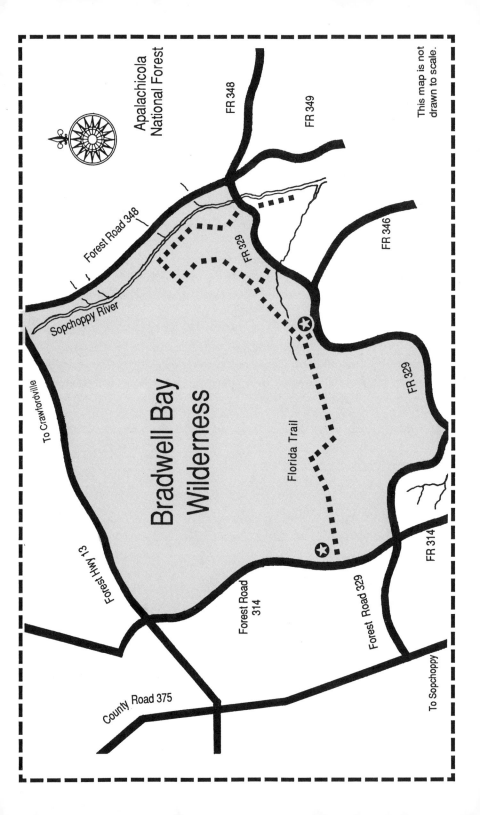

Bradwell Bay — Swamp Hike

It's a wet, wild and wonderful wilderness area

Any suggestion that a walk through a swamp might be a pleasant weekend diversion can sometimes produce an odd reaction. After all, swamps mean snakes, alligators, mud and mosquitoes. But swamps also mean towering, moss-laden cypress trees, jungle-like vegetation, abundant wildlife, and a chance to make contact with nature that just doesn't present itself in tamer outdoor pursuits.

A section of the Florida National Scenic Trail passes through the Bradwell Bay Wilderness Area in Apalachicola National Forest. The term "bay" describes a low-lying area, surrounded by slightly higher ground. At the heart of Bradwell Bay lies an undisturbed, primeval swamp, one of the largest in North Florida.

In 1975, the 24,600-acre area was designated as a National Wilderness Area and protected from all disturbing forms of intrusion such as road building or timber harvest. It's one of the largest wilderness areas in the eastern United States and gives visitors a chance to see a part of Florida as it was before European man arrived.

To fit the criteria of a wilderness area under the Wilderness Act passed by Congress in 1964, the bay had to be "an area where the earth and its community of life are untrammeled by man, where man himself is a visitor who does not remain." It is.

The entire section of trail passing through the Bradwell Bay Wilderness Area is about 15 miles long, but a convenient cutoff allows hikers to enjoy a six-mile section that passes through the center of the swamp, which is the most spectacular part of the bay.

The first part of the Bradwell Bay Trail, if you hike west from the cutoff, passes through pine flatwoods, characterized by longleaf pine, palmettos, and wiregrass.

A part of this section of the bay was burned in 1991 and offers the

17

hiker a chance to witness the rejuvenation of a forest after the natural process of fire. In the longleaf/wiregrass forest, fire is an important part of the ecosystem. The heat releases longleaf pine seeds from pine cones while the fire clears the ground for "planting." Ashes add fertilizer to the soil. Both longleaf pine and wiregrass have a built-in tolerance to fire which gives them an advantage over other species like hardwoods that are more likely to burn up.

A mile or so farther and the trail enters the swamp. This is the highlight of the hike. Because of the difficulty of reaching this area with machinery, the trees were never harvested. The average slash pine is over 100 years old and many of the cypress and hardwoods are 200 to 400 years old and include some magnificent specimens.

This is also the wettest part of the trail. You can encounter knee-deep water in the swamp even during dry times, and much deeper water conditions during rainy months. The rest of the trail is usually dry.

After leaving the swamp, the last mile of the trail follows an old tram road that represents some of the limited intrusion by lumber interests into the area earlier in the century. In places, the old rail bed is still visible. This open section of the trail contains a variety of insect-eating plants including sundews and pitcher plants.

Directions

From Crawfordville go west on Forest Highway 13 to Forest Road 314. Turn south for about 4.5 miles; you'll see a sign showing where the Florida Trail intersects the road. This is where you can drop a car.

Continue south a little over a mile to Forest Road 329; turn east and go about 7.7 miles. A small Bradwell Bay Wilderness Area sign with an orange blaze on it marks the beginning of the cutoff into the trail. About 100 yards from the road the cutoff trail intersects the Florida Trail. Turn left and you're headed for the swamp.

Orange blazes on trees a few feet above the ground mark the Florida Trail. When hiking through Bradwell Bay be sure to locate the next blaze before losing sight of the last one. This is not a nice place to be lost in. A double blaze means a sharp turn in the trail.

Note: The Bradwell Bay Wilderness Area is just that, a wilderness. Carry a map and a compass, and if possible, hike it the first time with someone that's familiar with the trail. When walking the trail from west to east, watch carefully for the cutoff trail that leads out to Forest Road 329. Also, it gets dark early beneath the thick canopy of the swamp, so allow for plenty of daylight for the hike.

Hikers in Bradwell Bay are always impressed by the sheer size of the 300-year-old pines scattered through the swamp forest.

For more information on Bradwell Bay contact the U.S. Forest Service, 325 John Knox Road, Suite F-100, Tallahassee, FL 32303, (904) 942-9300. Maps of Apalachicola National Forest can be obtained by sending $2.00 to the above address.

For more information on the Florida Trail contact the Florida Trail Association, P.O. Box 13708, Gainesville, FL 32604-1708, (800) 343-1882 or (904) 378-8823.

Elevated boardwalks and viewing platforms provide scenic opportunities without damaging the fragile sinks' environment.

Leon Sinks

A "hiker-friendly" geological area where you can easily spend an hour or a day

A few miles south of Tallahassee, in the Apalachicola National Forest, lies some of the most impressive geological formations in North Florida. Called the Leon Sinks Geological Area, it sports numerous large sink holes, a cave and a creek that disappears underground. In order to protect the unique formations, the 548-acre tract was designated as a Special Interest Area by the U.S. Forest Service in January, 1986. This designation allowed for the development of a management plan based upon Forest Service objectives and public input. The loop trail goes both north and south from the trailhead. The sinkhole trail is marked with blue blazes on tree trunks about five feet above the ground and travels north. If you start south, the trail is marked with green blazes. The first interesting formation you'll encounter is Gopher Hole Cave, which is actually a cavern with a submerged floor and a chimney.

Continuing south, the trail skirts the edge of a series of small tupelo swamps, some with scattered cypress trees. Further along, a section of trail follows Fisher Creek, which at one point drops underground for about 25 yards at a spot appropriately named Natural Bridge. A few hundred yards beyond that, Fisher Creek permanently disappears underground.

The trail continues past a number of sink holes, some dry, some filled with tannic-stained water, and a couple that reflect the blue sky in their crystal-clear waters.

Giant magnolia trees grow out of the dry basin of Magnolia Sink, which also contains a scattering of interesting limestone outcroppings. The tannic stained waters of Big Dismal Sink reveal its connection to surface waters. In contrast, the blue waters of Hammock Sink (also known locally as Little Dismal) reveal its connection to the Florida aquifer. Because of this connection, Hammock Sink offers world-class cave

21

diving as part of one of the largest known underground cave systems in the world.

A cross trail, marked with white blazes, turns off the main loop trail near Gopher Hole Cave and rejoins the main trail at Natural Bridge. This route shortens the loop trail by about one and a half miles and still allows you to see all the major sinks, although it misses the tupelo swamps.

Other forest types represented along the trail include a mixed hardwood forest, longleaf pine/wiregrass communities, and a titi thicket. There are approximately 10 varieties of oak in the sink area and the understory contains such common plants as rusty blackhaw, dogwoods, deerberry, sparkleberry, wild plum, and black cherry.

Depending upon the time of year, alert hikers will be rewarded with a glimpse of numerous bird species such as parula and pine warblers, summer tanagers, acadian flycatchers, great crested flycatchers, and pileated woodpeckers.

Facilities

There is ample parking, restrooms and drinking water at the trailhead. There are interpretive displays that explain the geology of the sinkholes and the ecological features in the area. Some trails are accessible to persons with disabilities. Leon Sinks is open year-round for day-use only. There is no entrance fee.

Directions

The entrance to the Leon Sinks Geological Area is located on U.S. Highway 319 (Crawfordville Highway), five-and-a-half miles south of Capitol Circle and nine miles north of Crawfordville.

For more information contact the U.S. Forest Service, 325 John Knox Road, Suite F-100, Tallahassee, 32303; (904) 942-9300. Maps of Apalachicola National Forest can be obtained by sending $2 to the above address.

For more information on the Florida Trail, which connects to the Leon Sinks Trail, contact the Florida Trail Association, P.O. Box 13708, Gainesville, FL 32604-1708; 1(800) 343-1882 or 1(904) 378-8823.

Signs and blazes on trees mark forested trails connecting the sinks and other geologic features.

Canoeing

Canoeing opportunities in the Big Bend area are so vast that it hardly seems fair to the rest of the state. Crystal-clear rivers spring from the ground and flow beneath spectacular tree canopies on their way to the rich, life-filled estuaries of the Gulf. There are also dark, tannin-stained streams that draw their water from cypress-shrouded swamps and cut narrow channels in the soft limestone bedrock. There's even a 160-year old canal dug for steamboats that still flows through the woods.

River birches, live oaks, magnolias, pines, sable palms, and palmetto bushes are among the plants that thrive on North Florida river banks. But it's the wildlife that adds so much to a Big Bend river experience. In wide, clear streams, wading birds come to sample the fish, and ducks come to feast upon the aquatic vegetation. Beneath forested canopies kingfishers fly low looking for minnows venturing too near the surface.

In all the rivers, largemouth bass hide beneath floating vegetation, turtles line up on fallen logs, and raccoons come to the bank to wet their food. If you move quietly you might see a deer or even a flock of turkeys venturing to the river for a drink.

Except for a couple short stretches of rapids on the Aucilla, most of the rivers are narrow, shallow and calm. A greater danger can exist during periods of heavy rain when the small rivers climb out of their banks. Paddlers on a flooded river can find themselves swept against the trees or over-turned against a snag.

Although incidents are very rare, keep well away from the large alligators. Also, keep an eye out for cottonmouth water moccasins. Don't place your hand on a tree trunk or fallen log without looking first.

Poison ivy grows profusely along many of the river banks, especially in low, moist areas. Also, in the summer, red wasps have a habit of building nests in bushes or tree branches that hang low over the water. Try to avoid paddling or drifting through any over-hanging vegetation.

Don't let these things keep you from exploring the rivers of the Big Bend, however, simply take precautions and always carry plenty of water, insect repellant, and a first aid kit.

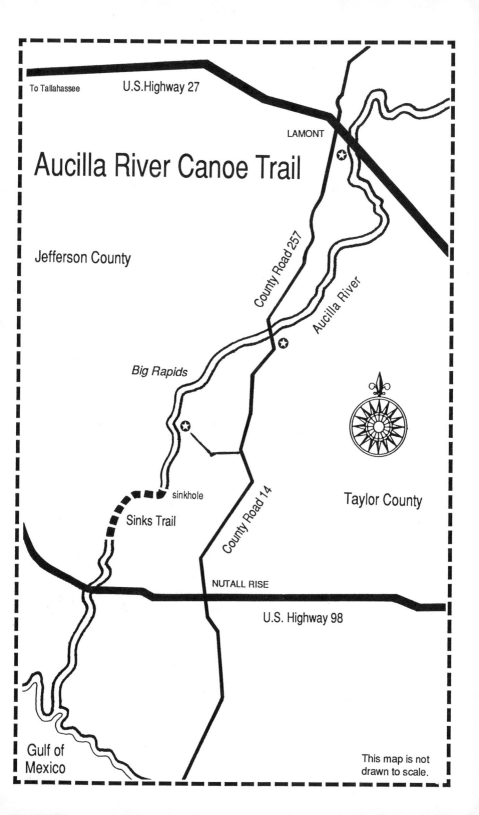

Aucilla River

Hardwood forest, swampy lowlands, and occassional rapids characterize this narrow river

Sandy banks with occasional limestone outcroppings line much of this small river which flows through an upland hardwood forest interspersed by sections of swampy lowland. Live oaks overhang the water, sharing the river bank with towering cypress trees and their attendant gathering of cypress knees which anchor the trees and help them breathe in the moist environment. River birches, pines, spruce trees, sable palms and a scattering of palmettos fill in much of the remaining forest floor. Watch for poison ivy along the shoreline.

The undeveloped banks of the Aucilla are home to an abundance of wildlife. Squirrels scurry through the overhead canopy, alligators and turtles slip into the river at the paddler's approach, and water moccasins bask in sunny spots along the bank. Anhingas, ibis, great blue herons, pileated woodpeckers, little blue herons, and kingfishers make their home in the forested river corridor.

The Aucilla originates in southern Georgia and flows 69 miles to the Gulf of Mexico. Above Highway 27 it's very narrow and difficult to navigate. Below the highway it becomes more of an established river within banks that stand up to eight feet high in places. About ten miles from the Gulf of Mexico the river is captured by a sink hole. It re-emerges five miles farther south near the small settlement of Nutall Rise. From there it flows another five miles to the Gulf. While underground the river's waters can be seen in a series of 16 sink holes. [See Aucilla Sinks Trail on page 13 for information on visiting these sinks.]

The Aucilla is very responsive to current rainfall conditions. During dry times it runs very shallow, and there are a few spots where you might have to step out and drag or carry your canoe. The rocky bottom can also redesign your paint job.

Other times after heavy rains in North Florida or South Georgia the river can flood well out of its banks. During these conditions the water swirls around one bend after another, pushing the novice paddler into one treetop after another. [See caution note below.]

Paddle Trips

A 19-mile section of the Aucilla, directly south of U.S. Highway 27 provides the best canoeing and kayaking opportunities. Easily accessible launching and take-out points divide this section into two trips.

13-Mile Trip — A 13-mile trip begins where U.S. 27 crosses the Aucilla about one mile east of the town of Lamont which is about 30 miles east of Tallahassee. To drop a car at the take-out point, take County Road 257 south from Lamont for eight miles to where it crosses the river. Plan to take the boat out at the south end of the bridge by the upstream side.

There are a few sets of mild rapids and short drops along this part of the river including the remnants of two limestone dams. Both are generally easy to negotiate, but can offer a slight challenge to the novice canoeist, especially during low water. However, if you're concerned at all, you can simply put ashore and carry the boat downstream a few yards to calmer water.

6-Mile Trip including "Big Rapids" — A second float trip begins where the first trip ended — at the County Road 257 bridge. It ends at a dirt landing about six miles down river. To get to the take-out point continue south from the bridge on County Road 257 for four miles to

where the pavement ends. Go a half-mile farther to the intersection of a broad dirt road. Turn right, and follow this road around a bend to the left for .7 of a mile. Turn right on a smaller road and follow it just over two miles to the river.

This section of river has a couple sets of rapids including Big Rapids, a true run of whitewater. If you're carrying a load of fishing tackle or cameras you might consider a portage. The rapids have claimed many a canoe. In any case, scout the rapids before attempting passage even if you're familiar with them.

Some of the dirt roads traveled to the take-out point for the lower trip can be rocky and bumpy but are usually passable for most cars. The roads near the river are prone to flooding during periods of heavy rainfall.

Caution

Misjudging the conditions on the Aucilla can turn an enjoyable outing into a bad experience. There's a water gauge under the east side of the U.S. 27 Bridge. If the level is below 5 1/2 feet you can expect to do a lot of bottom scraping. A level from 6 1/2 - 8 feet is ideal; and anything over 9 feet means the river is out of its banks and is considered to be unsafe.

St. Marks River

The St. Marks River above Natural Bridge is an often overlooked, paddling experience

The St. Marks River begins in wetlands east of Tallahassee and flows 35 miles to the Gulf. Along the way, numerous springs, the largest of which is Horn Springs, add their water to the stream by way of small creeks.

The St. Marks is one of the most historic rivers in the state, bearing witness to Spanish galleons, French and English pirates, indian raids, the invasion of Andrew Jackson, and a Civil War battle. Towns have sprung up along the banks only to succumb to hurricanes or economic disasters.

The most unusual feature of the river is Natural Bridge, a spot where the river flows underground for about 150 feet dividing the river into upper and lower sections.

While fishing boats, cabin cruisers, and oil barges ply the lower river, the shallow waters of the upper St. Marks is reserved for canoes and kayaks. The two-and-a-half mile section of the upper river, from Natural Bridge upstream to Horn Springs is easily passable by paddled watercraft. Above there the river is very narrow and often blocked by fallen trees.

Horn Springs can be reached overland if you want to travel one-way downstream, but the roads to it are rough and not maintained. The second sandy road to the left past Natural Bridge leads to the springs, but it should only be used by four-wheel drive vehicles. In addition, the tributary from Horn Springs to the river is thoroughly blocked by fallen trees.

The best approach is to paddle upstream from Natural Bridge then return downstream to your starting point. There are a number of convenient launching points next to the river just east of Natural Bridge. Most of the time, the current is fairly slow except after periods of heavy rain.

Heading upstream from Natural Bridge you're immediately surrounded by a mature hardwood forest. Giant bald cypress, magnolias, and live oaks form an intermittent canopy, filtering the sunlight through to the water. In fact, some of the finest specimens of cypress trees in the area can be seen along the banks.

There is also an occasional downed tree blocking the river that has to be dealt with. If you need to get out of the boat, the water is cold but the bottom is usually firm. Of course there's always the dry approach of stepping out on the log, pulling the canoe over, and climbing back in. Because of the lack of traffic on the river there is plenty of wildlife.

Wood ducks jump up and fly ahead of the boat, kingfishers chatter and dive for minnows, and you can often hear pileated woodpeckers pounding away deep in the woods.

There is also an abundance of small largemouth bass in the shallow river, and mullet that must have traveled through the underground passage to get there.

Prior to reaching the springs the river spreads out and is covered from bank to bank with a near solid mat of aquatic grasses. About 300 yards beyond the vegetation, the river forks. The right fork dwindles into a dead end. The left fork, which has a downed tree across the entrance, continues up river.

A short distance farther and the river forks again. At this point, the crystal-clear water flowing out of the right fork reveals it as the way to Horn Springs.

The final 300-foot run to the largest of the two springs is very narrow and blocked by a number of trees. It's not a bad idea to walk the last few yards.

The spring is 75 to 100 feet wide, and 20 to 30 feet deep. The blue-green waters are surrounded by high ground, including a small, sandy "beach" which makes an excellent picnic spot. A second, smaller spring lies a couple hundred feet to the south.

Like most of the Big Bend rivers, the St. Marks can climb out of it's low banks during periods of heavy rains. Caution is vital during high-water conditions.

Directions
The Natural Bridge State Historic Site is located six miles east of Woodville Highway (State Road 363) on Natural Bridge Road (in Woodville, Florida, just south of Tallahassee). The river flows underground just beyond the monument to the Battle of Tallahassee.

31

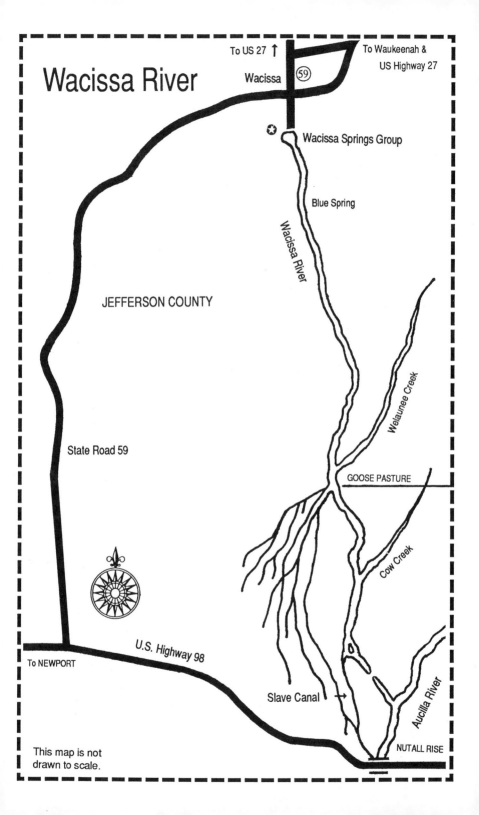

Wacissa River

The Wacissa is known for clear, spring-fed waters and abundant wildlife

In the early morning, a light fog rises from the cold waters of the Wacissa River. A pileated woodpecker rattles against a tree in the distance. Snowy egrets walk lightly across the vegetation while overhead a dozen scissor-tailed kites catch the first rising thermal currents of the day.

The Wacissa is one of the finest little rivers in Florida. The crystal-clear, spring-fed waters are full of fish and the low, swampy shoreline is covered with a mixture of cypress, oaks, tupelos, willows and pines. Deer are common along the river bank and the shallow water attracts a large number of wading birds. Turtles and alligators can always be seen basking on a convenient log.

The Wacissa is also a great place to spot a purple gallinule, one of Florida's most colorful birds. They can often be seen prowling around in the bull rushes and lily pads near shore.

The river arises fully formed from the Wacissa Springs Group which is located about one mile south of the town of Wacissa. From there it flows approximately 14 miles before joining the Aucilla River five miles from the Gulf of Mexico. There are three large springs at the headwaters and a dozen more scattered along the first mile of the river.

The largest spring, Blue Spring, is located about a mile downriver on the left. A short paddle down a small spring run brings you to this crystal-clear, circular pool, that's 90 feet wide with a middle depth of about 45 feet. Spanish moss-laden cypress trees surround the deep blue spring pool which must have been one of the main attractions when sightseeing boats toured the river around the turn of the century.

The clear waters of the Wacissa allow for a luxuriant growth of emergent and submergent aquatic vegetation. A nearly solid growth of eelgrass covers the river's bottom and waves continuously in the current. In many of the wider, shallow areas, including the headwaters, hydrilla

Much of the Wacissa River is wide and slow-moving with large mats of vegetation covering much of the surface.

has replaced much of the native eelgrass.

Navigation on the Wacissa is limited to canoes and small "riverboats." Canoes can travel the entire river, but power boats are stopped about mid-river by the remnants of an old railroad trestle.

There are two downstream canoe trips along the Wacissa. One from the headwaters to Goose Pasture and another from Goose Pasture to Nutall Rise by way of the Slave Canal. [See page 38 for more information on the Slave Canal.]

The entire river can be paddled in one day or you can camp overnight at Goose Pasture and proceed to Nutall Rise the following day. Another option is spending an enjoyable couple of hours exploring the headwater springs.

A small park at the headwaters of the river has a picnic table, a diving platform and a small concrete boatramp.

At Goose Pasture there's a small boat ramp, a few picnic tables and a wide grassy area beneath a scattering of giant live oaks. Camping is permitted all year except during hunting season.

The public ramp at Nutall Rise which largely accommodates boats using the lower Aucilla River is a convenient take-out point for canoeists paddling the Slave Canal.

Canoe Trips

Headwaters to Goose Pasture (9 miles)

At the beginning the river is wide and slow-moving with vegetation covering most of the surface. A clear stream near the east bank provides an unimpeded path through the aquatic vegetation.

Downstream the river alternates between wide slow-flowing sections and swift, narrow stretches that wind around small islands and between low banks. There are no rapids or obstacles along the way. The only break in the river is the remains of an old railroad trestle that has a gap in the center where small boats can pass.

Goose Pasture to Nutall Rise (5 miles)

About two miles downstream from Goose Pasture the river spreads into a myriad of swampy streams, a few of which apparently lead to the Aucilla River above the point where it drops underground.

35

A man-made extension of the Wacissa called the Slave Canal provides a way for canoeists to by-pass the swamp and reach the lower Aucilla River near Nutall Rise. (Please see the next chapter on page 40 for directions.) However, the entrance to the Slave Canal, which resembles a small stream, is difficult to find. Go with someone who knows the way your first time or two. More than one canoe party has become lost after missing the entrance.

Also expect to haul your canoe or kayak over an occasional downed tree.

When you reach the Aucilla River turn left (upstream) and paddle a few hundred yards to the boatramp at Nutall Rise. This section of the trip can have a strong current during high water conditions.

Directions
Headwaters
The headwaters of the Wacissa are located one mile south of the town of Wacissa. From Tallahassee take U.S. Highway 27 east then turn south on State Road 59. Continue straight when the highway route turns west. Or, take Tram Road from southeast Tallahassee straight to the town of Wacissa. Turn right at the intersection with State Road 59 and follow it straight south out of town to the river.

Goose Pasture
To reach Goose Pasture from Wacissa go south on State Road 59 to U.S. Highway 98 and turn left. Continue east for 1.5 miles to Limerock Industries Road, the second paved road past the bridge over the Aucilla River. Turn north and go 2.1 miles beyond the end of the pavement to an intersection of two dirt roads. Turn left again. At a fork in the road, bear left and you'll be heading straight into Goose Pasture.

Caution: The road to Goose Pasture can be rough and muddy at times, depending on recent rainfall. And on rare occasions it can be flooded. However, it is graded periodically and usually poses no problem to cars or trucks. (For a map to Goose Pasture see page 12.)

Nutall Rise
Nutall Rise is at the intersection of U.S. 98 and the Aucilla River. The boat ramp is located about a quarter mile north of the highway on a dirt road just east of the bridge.

Canoe Rentals

Canoes are available for rent every weekend at the headwaters by the hour or for one-way trips to Goose Pasture or Nutall Rise. The livery service also provides a shuttle back to your car for a slightly higher charge. For reservations or group trip information contact the Canoe Shop in Tallahassee at (904) 576-5335.

Goose pasture offers public camping with primitive facilities year-round except during hunting season.

The Slave Canal

*Time has worked its magic on the Slave Canal Canoe Trail,
a man-made extention to the Wacissa River*

Your senses have plenty to feast upon during a canoe trip along a canopied waterway like the Slave Canal. There's the feel of cool, moist air against your skin. There's the smell of clean, undisturbed water mixed with the earthy odor of rotting vegetation. And there are the sounds of the birds, insects and reptiles going about their daily routine.

But most importantly, there's the quality of light—soft, diffused sunlight, streaming through a covering of leaves like green, stained glass windows in a huge, open air cathedral.

The Slave Canal looks more like a natural stream than a canal.

Named for the fact that slaves were used in its construction, the Slave Canal connects the lower Wacissa to the Aucilla River near Nutall Rise.

It was in 1829 that surveyors discovered that the Wacissa River connected to the Aucilla River through a myriad of small streams. Since the Aucilla flowed from that point uninterrupted to the Gulf, a plan was formed to dig a canal connecting the two rivers so small cargo boats could reach the headwaters of the Wacissa from the Gulf of Mexico. To this end, the Wacissa and Aucilla Navigation Company was organized in 1831.

Construction of the canal took place sporadically during the 1830s and '40s, and as a result of indian conflicts, economic depressions, and the coming of the railroad, the project was finally abandoned in the early 1850s. Although a connection was made between the two rivers, no cargo boat was ever to make the journey from the Gulf to the headwaters of the Wacissa.

Little did the canal builders know that rather than leaving an unfulfilled promise of prosperity for the people of North Florida, they left a beautiful canoe trail that would allow future weekend explorers the opportunity to experience a little wilderness anytime they wished.

The canal is an easy paddle, with only an occasional pull-over, depending upon the water level. Since it was dug only deep enough to handle boats with less than 18 inches of draft, what remains is a shallow waterway ideal for canoes and kayaks.

It's hard to tell that the Slave Canal was even created by man. Time has worked its magic, and today it has the appearance of a natural stream. However, in some spots you can still see piles of boulders stacked along the shore by the original builders.

Seldom more than 15 feet wide, the canal flows through a swampy, hardwood forest of giant oaks, cypress, ash, and willow trees. In some places the paddler passes through sable palm hammocks dotted with cabbage palms, and palmetto bushes.

Alligators, gar, largemouth bass and turtles live in the clear, canal waters and an occasional water moccasin lies coiled in a sunny spot along the shore or on a downed log.

Birds are abundant along the canal. On a typical trip you might see prothonotary warblers, yellow-billed cuckoos, kingfishers, white ibis, and maybe a yellow-crowned night heron.

The hardest part about a trip down the Slave Canal is finding it. The entrance from the Wacissa River is somewhat hidden and during periods of heavy vegetative growth, can be difficult to locate.

When you head downstream from Goose Pasture, the Wacissa River soon narrows into a braided-stream system with a number of passable waterways. The best way through is to generally bear right whenever possible. Eventually the individual streams come back together and the river widens to about 50 feet. This is the last open section on the Wacissa. As the river begins to narrow again it forks left and right around a large patch of wild rice. The left fork continues into a swamp, forming another braided-stream system. This is the area you want to avoid.

The right fork, which is usually a small stream through the vegetation, continues straight for maybe 30-50 yards, then takes a hard right turn through some over-hanging trees. An iron post standing a few feet inside the wild rice on the left marks the spot. If it's your first trip, be sure you locate the signpost before venturing into what might or might not be the Slave Canal.

Once in the canal, the stream opens up, and turns left. You'll know you're in the right place by the rocks stacked along the bank. There's also an old tin hunting shack on the right side of the canal a short distance from the beginning.

An even better idea is to go with someone who knows the way the first time. More than once, canoe parties have missed the entrance and ended up spending a very uncomfortable night in the swamp. The best advice, and the only choice if you can't find the entrance is to return to Goose Pasture.

Directions

The take-out point on a trip through the Slave Canal is at Nutall Rise, which is 14.5 miles east of Newport, or just east of where the Aucilla River flows under U.S. Highway 98. Follow the dirt road from the highway a couple hundred yards to the boat ramp parking area where you can leave a vehicle.

The Slave Canal intersects the Aucilla River just below Nutall Rise. When you reach the end of the canal turn left, paddle upstream about 2,000 yards, and you'll come to the boat ramp.

Trips through the Slave Canal can begin at Goose Pasture (5-miles), or at the headwaters of the Wacissa (14-miles). For directions and canoe rental information see pages 36 & 37 in the chapter on the Wacissa River.

Wakulla River

The mysterious Wakulla flows forth from one of the largest springs in the world

The Wakulla is a clear, swampy, "Florida" river that rises from Wakulla Springs, the largest spring in Florida and one of the largest in the world. The headwater spring is located in the Edward C. Ball Wakulla Springs State Park.

Wakulla, which means "Mysterious Strange Water" is aptly named. Water pours forth from an underground cavern at a rate of 600,000 gallons of water per minute. The spring entrance is clearly visible 120 feet below the surface.

The upper river is fenced within the state park. The fence crosses the river a few yards upstream from the State Highway 365 bridge.

Access to the spring and upper river is only through the state park. Glass bottom boats circle over the four-and-a-half acre spring basin and tour boats travel the upper section of the river allowing visitors to view the abundant wildlife. There is no personal boat use within the park.

The is also a lodge and convention center next to the spring that was built in 1937 by industrial magnate Ed Ball. In the summer the cold, spring waters draw a crowd of swimmers. The lodge and restaurant still operates under the direction of the Florida State University School of Hotel and Restaurant Management.

The spring is famous for artifacts and fossils recovered from the spring's cave — including a Mastodon skeleton. The headwaters were also the site for the filming of a couple of Johnny Weismuller's *Tarzan* movies.

Wakulla Springs, in Wakulla Springs State Park, is a popular swimming hole during hot summer months.

Large alligators are a common sight on the Wakulla River.

For the next 10 miles, this broad, shallow river meanders between low swampy banks, until joining with the St. Marks River about six miles from the Gulf. Much of the river's "banks" blend into a wetland domain of cypress trees, live oaks, pines, wax myrtles, palms, and palmettos. Alligators lurk in quiet pools just off the river, and ospreys nest high in the treetops.

The river is heavily vegetated; dollar bonnets, water lilies, spatter-dock, hydrilla and eelgrass line either side of the river. About a mile above Highway 98 the river widens and becomes shallower and eelgrass and hydrilla become the more prevalent vegetation.

Despite the sometimes heavy weekend traffic, wildlife is usually abundant. Wading birds, kingfishers, and osprey are common, as are alligators and turtles which take advantage of every piece of dry land available. There are no facilities and few places to stop along the way.

In the summer, keep an eye out for manatees which spend the hot months in the cool, spring-fed water, grazing on their favorite selections of underwater vegetation.

Canoe Trip

The Wakulla River Canoe Trip consists of an easy paddle from the State Road 365 bridge, three-and-a-half miles downstream to the U.S. Highway 98 bridge.

The upper bridge, on State Road 365, is about two miles west of Woodville Highway (State Highway 363), south of Tallahassee.

There is some limited parking at the upper bridge and a small, dirt ramp. At Highway 98 there is also limited parking and a small, paved ramp.

A canoe livery located next to the lower bridge rents canoes for an upstream/downstream canoe trip. The current is fairly easy to paddle against.

The entrance to Wakulla Springs State Park is near the intersection of State Road 61 and State Road 267.

For information contact: Edward C. Ball Wakulla Springs State Park, Wakulla Springs Road, Wakulla Springs, FL 32305. Call (904) 922-3632 for information on boat tours and nature trails or (904) 224-5950 for accommodations at the lodge.

For information on canoe rentals contact: TNT Hideaway, Highway 98, St. Marks, FL 32355; (904) 925-6412. The canoe livery is located on the shores of the Wakulla River at Highway 98.

Biking in the Big Bend

Bicycling enthusiasts are enjoying a steady growth in opportunities throughout the Big Bend partially due to a growing national trend, and partially because of the varied, and wonderful old and new trails available in the area.

Shady, lightly-traveled, canopy roads and rural highways follow the contour of the rolling red clay hills through the surrounding countryside. Hundreds of miles of unpaved forest roads invite the off-road enthusiast and the dikes of the St. Marks National Wildife Refuge offer wonderful riding and wildlife viewing adventures. The Tallahassee-St. Marks Historic Railroad State Trail, a rails to trails project created by the State of Florida, is used by thousands of riders every week.

Capital City Cyclists, is an energetic organization with a steady schedule of rides for both conventional and off-road enthusiasts. There are rides for beginners, intermediates and advanced cyclists. The club newsletter, published by-monthly, helps keep cyclists informed of club news, cycling tips and includes a calendar of upcoming rides.

For more information contact Capital City Cyclists, P.O. Box 4222, Tallahassee, FL 32315-4222.

"Train depot" trailhead is a tribute to the St. Marks Trail's original purpose.

Tallahassee-St. Marks Historic Railroad State Trail

From the day the Tallahassee-St. Marks Historic Railroad State Trail opened in 1988, thousands of people each month have been using the 16-mile stretch of old railroad bed for hiking, jogging, horseback riding, bicycling, or just taking a stroll on a summer's evening. Why not, it's an inviting opportunity to travel through the woods instead of along a busy highway.

The majority of trail travelers are bicycle riders. You learn why right after you start your first trip. Remember when you were a kid on a bicycle, there was nothing more inviting than a long, smooth stretch of pavement with no cars, no trucks, no curbs, no stop lights. What a thrill it was to peddle up to speed, then cruise along with the wind against your face. Remember how much fun that was and how free it made you feel? Well it still is, and it still does, and you find that out as soon as your feet hit the peddles.

This was the first Rails to Trails project in Florida, which is appropriate since it takes the place of the first railroad line chartered in Florida and the first railroad in the nation to receive a federal land grant.

Completed in 1837, the railroad line connected Tallahassee with the shipping port of Port Leon. The line carried agricultural products, mainly cotton, from the interior of North Florida and South Georgia. In later years it carried timber and naval stores from the turpentine industry.

The railroad closed after 147 years, making it the longest operating railroad in Florida.

Directions

The trail starts at a parking lot on State Road 363, just south of Capital Circle (U.S. Highway 319). A small shelter in the shape of a miniature train platform marks the spot. From there it's 16.2 miles to the

47

trail's end at the town of St. Marks. The original railroad continued across the St. Marks River at this point.

Along most of the way the trail is bordered either by the forest or at least a buffer of trees that includes loblolly, longleaf and slash pines, live oaks, laurel oaks, and dogwoods. In the understory are plants like fetter bush, persimmons, blackberry, sumac, runner oak, and a variety of wildflowers.

A mile and a quarter south of the trailhead the Munson Hills Off-Road Bicycle Trail turns off into Apalachicola National Forest. The off-road trail takes a seven-and-a-half mile loop through the forest. (See Munson Hills Off-Road Bicycle Trail on page 50.)

Another side trip turns off in the small town of Woodville five miles south of the trailhead. The Natural Bridge Battlefield Historic Site is located six miles east of Woodville on Natural Bridge Road. The Civil War battle for Tallahassee took place at this spot where the St. Marks River flows underground for 150 feet forming a natural bridge.

Six and a half miles below Woodville, Highway 267 provides a side trip to Wakulla State Park five miles to the west. Wakulla Lodge and Springs is only about a mile inside the park entrance. You can take a dip in the cold spring waters, or have breakfast or lunch in the lodge's restaurant or snack bar.

The section of St. Marks Trail between Highway 267 and Highway 98 offers some excellent wildflower viewing opportunities, especially in the spring. Also watch along the east side of the trail for a large pine tree that still has a scarred tree trunk and part of a collecting pan left over from the turpentine collecting days.

The forest pattern also changes along this section of trail. The scenery begins to alternate between pine-palmetto communities on the uplands and small wetlands with titi, magnolia, and bald cypress trees.

The trail ends in St. Marks near a couple of restaurants and a small store. Fort San Marcos de Apalache offers a nice side trip of about one mile. Turn west and follow the paved road to an intersection with another paved road. The fort is a few hundred yards down the road to the left. A small museum stands at this spot which historically has been under the control of four nations: Spain, Britain, The Confederacy and the U.S.

Just because there's no cars on the trail that doesn't relieve the need for some safety precautions. Cyclists should watch for and obey traffic signs at intersections of the trail and roads. They should also stay on the right-hand side of the trail and signal their intention to pass when overtaking another rider or pedestrian.

The trail is owned by the Department of Transportation and is managed as a state park by the Department of Environmental Protection, Division of Recreation and State Lands.

For more information about the St. Marks-Tallahassee Historic Railroad State Trail contact Edward Ball Wakulla Springs State Park, Wakulla Springs Road, Wakulla Springs, FL 32305. Brochures with a map are usually available at the trailhead.

Cyclelogical Bike Shop, located at the north end of the trail, has bicycles and skates for sale or rent and sponsors some bicycle tours. Call (904) 656-0001 or write to Cyclelogical, 4780 Woodville Highway, Tallahassee, FL 32311.

Munson Hills Off-Road Bicycle Trail

The Munson Hills Trail passes through a longleaf pine forest.

The Munson Hills Off-Road Bicycle Trail in Apalachicola National Forest south of Tallahassee is an inviting system of trails that loop through a variety of forest habitats.

The various trails begin and end about 1.25 miles south of the trailhead of the Tallahassee-St. Marks Historic Railroad State Trail (better known as the St. Marks Bike Trail).

There's a sign posted above the paved trail marking the turn onto the Munson Hills Trail and into the national forest.

The actual off-road trail begins a couple hundred yards into the woods. It's a narrow, winding, path that twists and turns through the trees. There are small, log jumps placed along some sections to increase the trail's technical difficulty. The bike path also zigzags through a couple small groves of tightly spaced trees.

The trail's surface stays fairly well-packed during periods of regular rainfall. During dry times some of the sandier stretches can be soft; during rainy-periods a portion of the trail is muddy. Nevertheless, the Forest Service requests that you remain on the trail — "dismount and walk if necessary" — to protect the surrounding vegetation.

Blue blazes painted on tree trunks a few feet above the ground mark the main seven-and-an-half mile loop. A double blaze forewarns a sharp turn. The white-blazed cross trail, dubbed the Tall Pine Short Cut by Forest Service personnel, makes a return loop that creates a four-and-a-quarter mile-long trail.

Much of the Munson Hills Trail passes through a mature longleaf pine/wiregrass habitat. Along the way it also leads the cyclist through dense live-oak hammocks and along the edges of wet-season ponds. A series of low sand hills give the trail its name.

The project was developed by a local organization, the Fat of the Land Off-Road Bicycle Club (the term "Fat" refers to the wide tires used on the off-road bicycles) in cooperation with the United States Forest Service.

Recently, a primitive toilet, benches and a six-panel interpretive display have been added at the head of the Munson Hills Trail. The completed trail project will eventually connect the Blue Sink Recreation Area on Crawfordville Highway to the St. Marks Trail. The Forest Service plans to provide interpretive signs along the way that will describe the unique habitats, geological features and wildlife viewing opportunities.

You can rent off-road bicycles at the head of the St. Marks Trail near the intersection of Woodville Highway and Capital Circle. For information contact Cyclelogical at (904) 656-0001.

For a brochure of the trail write to: U.S. Forest Service, Wakulla Ranger District, Route 6, Box 7860, Crawfordville, Florida 32327.

Biking the Dikes

and other bicycling opportunites in the St. Marks
Wildlife Refuge (see map on page 84)

The chance to observe a variety of habitats and wildlife attracts
visitors to the St. Marks Wildlife Refuge.

If you're tired of riding in the neighborhood, or want a change from the Tallahassee-St. Marks Bike Trail consider driving a little farther south and unloading your bicycle in the St. Marks National Wildlife Refuge.

The refuge has dozens of miles of walking trails and 18 miles of impoundment dikes that are all open to the off-road bicycle enthusiast. In addition, some dikes are hard-packed enough for regular skinny-tire bicycles.

Tram road is one of the best trails for bicycles of either type. Bordered by forests, the single lane road runs 12 miles to a bridge over the Pinhook River.

The Deep Creek and Stoney Bayou Primitive Walking Trails are among the most scenic in the refuge. At one point the 12-mile Deep Creek Trail passes by a wilderness area and saltmarsh on the left and a freshwater marsh on the right.

All three trails, including the six-mile-long Stoney Bayou Trail, begin at a trailhead about a mile past the visitor center.

The Impoundments

The refuge dikes surround a series of impoundments that were created in the 1930s and subdivided in the 70s. The main purpose of the pools is to provide habitat for the thousands of migrating waterfowl that visit the Gulf coast every winter. In summer the pools are home to a wide sampling of North Florida's resident wildlife including alligators, anhingas, great blue herons, egrets and rails.

All of the interconnecting dikes are open for hiking and bicycles, although some are less suitable for bikes because of a rough or sandy surface. Trail choices should depend upon your level of off-road experience, and degree of stamina.

One of the smoothest dikes surrounds Stoney Bayou Pool Number 1. The two-and-a-half to three mile trip starts at a spot called "Double Dikes" which is where two parallel dikes intersect the main road directly across from the East River Pool.

Begin by following the right-hand dike, and turn right at every opportunity. You'll follow the perimeter of the impoundment and return to the road about half a mile from the starting point.

Watch for bald eagles and osprey perched on the lone trees standing out in the water and look for alligators near shore. Sometimes you can spot deer in the fields north of the dikes, especially early in the morning and late in the evening.

If you prefer "on-road" peddling, the main road leading to the lighthouse can provide much of the same fine scenery. You can park at the headquarters building or at any number of parking areas along the way. It's seven miles from the visitor center to the lighthouse.

Pick up a map of the refuge trails at the Visitor Center just inside the

The impoundments are a permanent home to a large variety of wading birds and a seasonal home to numerous migrating species.

entrance, and check with refuge personnel about current conditions on various trails.

Cautions

Be sure and carry plenty of water. There is no water available on any of the trails and no shade on the dikes. The only water in the refuge is at the Visitor Center.

Anytime other than mid-winter, plan for a lot of mosquitos and no-see-ums, especially at dawn and dusk. Apply you're favorite choice of insect repellant before starting out and take some extra with you. Mosquitoes can bite all day long in the refuge on days when there is little wind.

Also, if you sit in the grass during the summer without protection, you can expect to end up with an unpleasant case of chiggers.

An opportunity for a close-up view of wildlife is part of the attraction of the refuge dike system.

The wildlife refuge is open during daylight hours only. The Visitor Center is open Monday through Friday 8 a.m. to 4:15 p.m.; and Saturday and Sunday 10 a.m. to 5 p.m.

A Federal Duck Stamp, or Golden Eagle Pass is required for entrance into the St. Marks Refuge. One stamp or pass covers everybody in your car. You can also pay $3.00 per car every time you enter. Or if you choose to leave your car at the Visitor Center, you will only be charged the normal fee for entering on a bicycle, which is $1.

The St. Marks Refuge Association is a non-profit organization, whose members work with refuge personnel on projects ranging from the creation of hiking trails to writing plant and animal guides. They also take part in educational programs and guided tours in the refuge.

For more information on the association or the refuge contact St. Marks National Wildlife Refuge, P.O. Box 68, St. Marks, FL 32355; 904-925-6121.

State Parks

There are dozens of state parks in this region of North Florida; too many to cover in this publication without it becoming just a book about state parks. Instead we've included information about five of the area's parks that we've found to be the most interesting.

Florida state parks are managed to maintain the environment in a native condition while providing passive recreational opportunities to the public. Most parks provide camping, picnicking, hiking and wildlife viewing opportunities. Others add fishing, snorkeling, scalloping, and horseback riding to the list.

Habitats range from world-class beaches to some of the last remnants of the longleaf pine/wiregrass forest that once covered much of the southeastern United States. Every one of Florida's state parks contains something special. We recommend that you never pass one by without at least a brief visit.

For more information on state parks contact the Department of Environmental Protection, Division of Recreation and Parks, Office of Public Relations, 3900 Commonwealth Boulevard, M.S. #535, Tallahassee, FL 32399; (904) 488-9872.

The caves at Florida Caverns State Park hold a wonderful assortment of limestone formations.

Florida Caverns State Park

A climax forest and a wondrous system of caves makes this one of Florida's most unique state parks

The tour guide unlocks the big iron door at the bottom of the stairs and the small group of visitors begin their chilly, underground journey. Working their way through large rooms and along narrow passageways the cave "explorers" move deeper into the earth.

Every room is decorated with a new array of rock formations. Like looking for animal shapes in the puffy white clouds on a summer day, the remarkable formations are fuel for the imagination.

The shapes have proper names: stalactites, stalagmites, columns, rimstone, draperies, and sodastraws, but it's more fun to picture New York City hanging upside down or a miniature petrified forest, or perhaps even the face of Richard Nixon.

Clear pools of water perfectly reflect the limestone protrusions in the roof of the cave. The water is so clear and still, it could be ten feet deep or only inches.

The 1,783-acre Florida Caverns State Park encompasses a spectacular climax forest on the surface and a myriad of caves below ground.

The caves were formed in a 60,000,000-year-old bed of limestone that was deposited when this land was beneath the sea. The protective shells of sea creatures made up this rock layer which underlies the entire peninsula of Florida.

As the oceans retreated, the water table dropped to levels even lower than today. Ground water draining through forest plant litter became slightly acidic allowing it to dissolve the limestone as it worked its way underground.

Eventually, caverns were formed that are accessible where the limestone is exposed to the surface. Many of the caverns in the same layer of limestone throughout Florida are underwater during the current ocean levels; but in the "Florida Mountains" west of Tallahassee at least some of these caves are high and dry.

There are actually two levels of caves in the state park, a dry upper level and a flooded lower level. Geologists believe that another layer of caves once existed above the current ground level but they have already eroded away.

Water that continues to trickle into the caves is responsible for creating many of the formations that adorn the walls, floors and ceilings. When the limestone-laden water evaporates it leaves behind a small amount of a mineral called calcite which slowly builds into the various shapes.

The largest cave is lighted, and was made accessible to the general public by the Civilian Conservation Corps in the 1930s. Most of the other thirty or so caves are closed to protect the formations and the wildlife. Bats, cave salamanders, crickets and crawfish are among the animals that inhabit this unusual environment.

Other Park Treats

The Chipola River flows through Florida Caverns State Park. At one point the small, winding river takes its own journey underground for a few hundred yards. The spot is appropriately named Natural Bridge.

There's also a short but very impressive nature trail that winds through a magnificent example of a climax forest of giant magnolias, beeches, white oaks and dogwoods. Even if the caves didn't exist, the forest would be worth the trip.

During the spring, wildflowers brighten the landscape. Trillium, columbine, Damascus lilies, wild roses and phlox are scattered throughout the forest floor.

The trail also passes through a short cave, and follows a high limestone bluff along Spring Branch, a tributary of the Chipola. Small cave entrances and eroded cliffs add to the interesting sites along the hiking trail.

The nature trail at Florida Caverns State Park is alive with colorful wildflowers in the early spring.

The park is located outside of Marianna, about 65 miles west of Tallahassee.

The caverns are chilly, maintaining a steady temperature of around 58 degrees. The main tour takes about 45 minutes. There is no unguided exploration of the caverns allowed. There is a charge for the cave tour. A short movie and educational displays at the park's visitor center explain the formation of the caverns and the climax forest.

The park also has camping, swimming, picnicking, fishing, canoeing, and horse trails.

For more information contact Florida Caverns State Park, 2701 Caverns Road, Marianna, FL 32446; (904) 482-9598.

From St. Joe State Park — a view of the shallow waters of St. Joe Bay.

St. Joe State Park

St. Joe Bay and one of the world's finest beaches makes this park special

An "outdoor playground" is the best way to describe the T.H. Stone Memorial St. Joseph Peninsula State Park.

Regardless of your favorite recreational pursuits, you're bound to find something to do; kayaking, fishing, boating, sunbathing, swimming, snorkeling, hiking and birdwatching. It's all there.

The park takes up the northern 2,516 acres of the St. Joseph Peninsula, a large sandy spit with the Gulf of Mexico on one side and St.

The shaded campgrounds in the park are located within walking distance of the beach and the bay.

Joe Bay on the other. The peninsula extends from the mainland about 20 miles west of Apalachicola.

The interior of the park contains a scattering of freshwater marshes and old dunes covered with oak and sand pine communities. An impressive dune formation separates the interior from the beach, and a saltwater marsh fringes much of the bay side.

St. Joe Bay is what makes the park special. The water is perpetually clear and there's a lush growth of seagrass that brings with it a wonderful variety of sea life. It's almost as if someone grabbed a piece of the Florida Keys and dropped it in the Florida Panhandle.

Snorkeling in the bay reveals an underwater world that's home to sea urchins, starfish, giant whelks, snails, and even an occasional octopus. But it's the opportunity to harvest a meal or two of fresh scallops that draws the most snorklers in the summer.

If you have a boat, there's a ramp and a boat basin in the park. You can also find scallops by wading out from the shore. Many waders tow a cooler or bucket to pile their catch in. Some of the best scalloping grounds are in the southern portion of the bay, but they can be plentiful just about anywhere there's seagrass.

You need a saltwater license to harvest scallops in Florida waters if you use any type of diving apparatus such as a snorkel. In addition, all divers must display a "Diver Down" flag, even if you walk out from shore. Scallop season currently opens on July 1 and closes October 1. [Be sure to check the current fishing regulations published by the Florida Marine Fisheries Commission for changes in dates and laws!]

The park has facilities for tents and camping vehicles. There are also eight cabins facing the bay that can be rented by the day or week. You can keep your boat in the water by the cabin, but you'll have to anchor well offshore because of the shallow water.

Each cabin has a screened-in porch facing the bay, just in case your recreational desires only extend to a comfortable chair with a good view.

The waters immediately out from the cabins produce good seatrout fishing during the summer. Look for areas with intermittent sandy spots and grass beds. The fish will be concentrated over the grassy areas.

On the other side of the park, past some of the tallest sand dunes in Florida, is a world-class beach with plenty of room for sunbathers and fishermen. The beach extends for about seven miles beyond the day-access area near the parking lot.

The white sand beach has been cited by the Laboratory for Coastal Research as one of the best beaches along the Gulf of Mexico. The entire upper 1,650 acres of the peninsula, called St. Joseph Spit on some maps, is designated a wilderness preserve. No land vehicles are allowed, but you can hike in and take advantage of the primitive camping. Boaters, including canoers and kayakers can launch in the park, ride up the bay and camp on the beach. Registration with park headquarters is required before camping.

There are also hiking trails in the park and the wilderness preserve. You can walk along the beach, the bayshore or the center of the peninsula. The trails are a great way to take advantage of the birdwatching opportunities. Over 200 species have been identified within the park's boundaries. The best birding times are during the spring and fall migration periods when everything from hawks to warblers stop over for a brief rest during their journey.

The park is located on Florida Highway 30, off U.S. Highway 98, a few miles west of Apalachicola.

For information or reservations for cabins or camping contact St. Joseph Peninsula State Park, Star Route 1, Box 200, Port St. Joe, FL 32456; (904) 227-1327.

Surf fishing at St. George Island State Park.

St. George Island State Park

Miles and miles of beautiful beaches make this park a popular destination

St. George Island State Park, which is mostly known for its magnificent beaches, encompasses the eastern 1,883 acres of St. George Island. Snow white, drifting sand dunes and a wide beach stretch for nine miles through the park.

The Laboratory for Coastal Research ranks the beaches of St. George Island State Park as one of the top ten beaches in the United States. Six hundred and fifty beaches were compared in the study.

There are generally three types of people entering the park on any given day — sunbathers, birders, and fishermen.

One paved road traverses the park along the north side of the beach dunes. A number of boardwalks leading from small parking lots provide access to the beach without damaging the delicate vegetation which holds the dunes in place.

There is also a large pavilion that provides some limited facilities for those seeking a tamer beach.

The park is also well-known for excellent surf-fishing opportunities. Every year, about the time sunbathers begin crowding the beaches, gamefish of all types begin gathering in the waters around the island.

The first to show up in the spring are Spanish mackerel, with an attendant scattering of bluefish. Next come migrating pompano running past the beaches on their way east, while at the same time whiting invade the shallow waters beneath the waves. Finally, seatrout and redfish arrive ready for action in the warming waters.

East Pass, between the east end of St. George Island and Dog Island might be the best fishing spot on the island. The currents pulling between the two islands attract both baitfish and gamefish.

The pass is at the east end of St. George Island State Park. In 1993, the Florida Department of Natural Resources instituted a $40.00 daily permit, or an $80.00 yearly permit to use a four-wheel drive vehicle to drive to East Pass from the end of the paved road. As an alternative, you can park at the end of the paved road and walk along the beach about a mile-and-a-half to the pass.

A less expensive, high-percentage fishing choice for a day in the sun is to fish for whiting in the surf anywhere along the island's beaches. The approach to catching whiting is to fish close to shore and stay alert. When these ever-hungry, cooperative fish swarm on a piece of shrimp it doesn't last long. If you're not paying attention you'll soon be fishing with a bare hook.

Whiting are an excellent choice for teaching children how to fish. They are small enough to catch on the lightest tackle, are easy to hook, and they hang around close to shore.

To catch other gamefish from the beach it's often necessary to wade out to the sandbar that runs along the beach and cast offshore from there. Seatrout, Spanish mackerel, bluefish, pompano, redfish and sharks can all be caught from the waters beyond the sandbar. Strips or chunks of cut mullet fished on the bottom is a good all-around bait for any of these species.

There are two tackle stores on St. George Island that sell frozen bait and other supplies for fishing off the beach. A saltwater license is not required for Florida residents when fishing from shore.

Birds

Over 100 species of birds have been identified in the park. Snowy plovers, least terns, black skimmers, willets and other shorebirds nest along the beaches and in the grassy marsh flats. Osprey and a variety of sea gulls are commonly seen. The open spaces and pine forests in the park are great places to view migrating birds during the spring and fall.

Facilities

The park has two sandy boat ramps for launching small boats into the bay. There's also camping at designated sites, picnic and swimming facilities and a couple hiking trails to choose from. Of course you can always hike along the beach.

A four-mile bridge and causeway connects St. George Island to the mainland in Eastpoint, Florida. During the spring and summer, large

Every spring Spanish mackerel gather to feed around the east end of St. George Island.

numbers of shorebirds including black skimmers, seagulls, and least terns (an endangered species) nest in the narrow strip of sand between the road and the seawall.

Please drive carefully and obey the speed limits when the birds are nesting. A cooperative effort between state and federal agencies and people driving over the causeway is helping to protect the birds.

Many of these same species also nest near the dunes along the beaches. Be careful during nesting season and stay near the water when walking the beach.

Directions

The park is approximately 75 miles west of Tallahassee. Take U.S. Highway 319 (Crawfordville Highway) to U.S. Highway 98, then west to Eastpoint (near Apalachicola). This is the scenic route; it follows the Gulf shoreline for many miles. There are numerous good restaurants and small fishing towns along the way.

There's an entrance fee to the park. For more information contact St. George Island State Park, P.O. Box 62, Eastpoint, Florida 32328; (904) 927-2111 or (904) 670-2111.

The inviting white sand beaches of Cape St. George Island can only be reached by boat.

Cape St. George Island State Preserve

If you have a boat, camping on the beach at Cape St. George State Preserve is a great way to spend a weekend in the spring or fall. Granted, it may be a little harder to go camping out of a boat than a car, but the benefits of having miles of undeveloped beach all to yourself far exceed the extra effort.

Also known locally as Little St. George Island, this barrier island is located due west of St. George Island and is part of the Apalachicola National Estuarine Research Reserve. Before the construction of Bob Sikes Cut in 1954, Cape St. George was actually a part of St. George Island.

If you're new to beach camping, a few extra supplies can help make camping on a beach an enjoyable experience. A tarp or beach umbrella will give you an occasional, much-needed break from the sun. Also, insect repellant for mosquitoes and a supply of Avon's Skin-So-Soft for the no-se-ums will come in handy if there is a warm spell.

If you plan to do any fishing, sand spikes will come in real handy. You'll be able to set the rod down without getting sand in the reel while you sit back and wait for the fish. Shrimp or cut mullet is a good, portable bait.

Just because you're camping on an island, however, doesn't mean the entertainment has to be restricted to fishing. There's ten miles of pristine Gulf beaches open to shelling. Anyone who enjoys collecting shells knows what a thrill it is to make the only set of footprints between the tides.

You don't have to give up the forest to camp on the beach either. The pine flatwoods and savannas on Cape St. George are crisscrossed with roads and trails that lead the explorer into a piece of original Florida.

If you like birding, the best time to camp is during the spring and fall migration. Birds are abundant and you stand a chance of seeing a bald eagle or an endangered peregrine falcon. In the summer, snowy plovers and oyster catchers nest on the beach.

There are designated camp sites at each end of the island open to the general public, one at West Pass and one at Bob Sikes Cut. Camping at either site is entirely primitive. You have to take everything you need, including fresh water. If the days are still hot, the standard rule is to take at least one gallon of water per person per day.

It's somewhat difficult to anchor a boat in the pass at the west end of the island but it can be done with a good anchor and a little caution. The current is swift and strong everywhere in the pass. At the east end of the island there is a small cove north of the jetty wall that offers some protection for an anchored boat.

There's a group campsite near the Government Dock on the bay side that can be used with permission. There's also a cabin on the bay that's closed to the general public but is available for environmental education and research groups.

It's also a good idea to remember that barrier islands serve as shock absorbers to protect the mainland from storm winds and waves. Unfortunately, this also means that there's little protection for a campsite on the exposed beach. Some extra rope and a few extra stakes will come in handy in keeping a tent in place against the wind. In addition, replacing regular tent stakes with stakes at least 18 inches long will anchor your tent more securely in the loose sand.

Directions

The boat ramp nearest West Pass and Bob Sikes Cut is the paved, public ramp in the city of Apalachicola near the foot of the bridge. A channel is marked to Bob Sikes Cut. West Pass is approximately nine miles to the west between Cape St. George Island and St. Vincent Island. A local Coast Guard chart of the area will help with navigation in Apalachicola Bay. U.S. Coast Guard Chart #11401 covers Apalachee Bay to Cape San Blas and is available in some local tackle stores and marinas.

Camping at West Pass at the west end of Cape St. George Island State Preserve.

As part of the Apalachicola National Estuarine Research Reserve (ANERR), Cape St. George State Preserve is managed by the Department of Environmental Protection, in cooperation with the Game and Fresh Water Fish Commission. All it takes to get permission to camp on the island is a phone call to ANERR at 904-653-8063, to let them know you'll be on the island.

In fact, you might want to stop by the Reserve headquarters in Apalachicola to pick up a map and a little information about the island, its history, and the role it plays in the overall estuarine system. The Apalachicola National Estuarine Research Reserve is located at 261, 7th Street, Apalachicola, FL 32320; (904) 653-8063.

To drive there continue straight when you come off the bridge into the town of Apalachicola. When the road dead-ends into a marina, turn left. The Reserve headquarters is on the left side at the end of the short road. The offices, and a public education facility called the Estuarine Walk is open weekdays from 8 a.m. to 5 p.m.

The historic Gregory house sits on a high bluff overlooking the Apalachicola River.

The rare Torreya tree is scattered throughout the park. This specimen is in the picnic area.

Torreya State Park
... a land rich with Deep South history

Torreya State Park might well be the most unique state park in Florida. It's actually a little piece of the Appalachian mountains tucked quietly in a remote spot of North Florida.

Viewing the Apalachicola River from the 220-foot-high river bluffs, it's not hard to imagine the passing riverboats that once carried the products of the Deep South to the town of Apalachicola, and on to the ports of the world during the last century.

The old steamboats weren't "paddle-wheel queens" like the ones on the Mississippi, they were boats built to carry cargo down a shallow river. They had small cabins, lots of deck space, and no ballrooms.

The deep ravines, the river, and the high bluffs are only part of the story of Torreya. Another story started about 12,000 years ago, during the last ice age, when the cold and ice moved south pushing northern species of plants and animals ahead of it. When the climate warmed up again these species followed the ice back north, but in some places small patches of northern vegetation remained behind.

The Appalachian-type forests of the park are a prime example of this phenomenon. Among the plants normally found farther north in the Appalachian Mountains are wild hydrangea, mountain laurel, and Carolina silver bell trees.

There are also a number of rare plants found only in this area including the torreya tree, the Florida yew, croomia (which is a small flowering plant), and the schisandra vine that is one of the oldest known flowering plants.

Because of this mixture of rare and out-of-place plants the forests of Torreya are often described as the most colorful in Florida when autumn colors set-in. The local belief is that the best colors occur in years when there's a frost before the end of October.

The best way to appreciate this environment so unique to Florida is to hike the seven-mile loop trail that winds around the perimeter of the 1,000-acre park. The trail passes through ravines and climbs over hills and across streams. It also runs along the river and across the high river bluffs. Along the way, you'll pass through distinct environmental communities like river swamps, pinelands, and hardwood hammocks.

Actually Torreya offers a great opportunity for beginning hikers and backpackers. The trails aren't long, and except for an occasional climb, aren't very difficult. The loop trail is laid out so you can walk one section at a time. One popular approach is to drop a car by the trail near the park entrance, then drive to another access point and hike back to the dropped car.

Two locations along the loop trail are designated as primitive camping areas for backpackers. The Rock Creek camp looks over Rock Creek, and the Rock Bluff Camp provides an excellent view of the Apalachicola River from a 200-foot-high vantage point. All overnight backpackers must register before heading out.

Bluffs Trail

The most popular walk is the Apalachicola River Bluffs Trail, a federally designated National Recreation Trail that encompasses part of the loop trail. Slightly less than a mile long, it gives the inexperienced or out-of-shape hiker a chance to see many of the geological formations and unique plant communities in the park.

The River Bluffs Trail begins and ends at the Gregory House, a restored pre-Civil War plantation home. Park rangers provide regular tours of the house and an explanation of plantation life.

As you walk the bluffs trail, it becomes evident that different elevations and moisture conditions allow for different mixtures and types of plants. The uplands at the head of the trail are a pine, scrub oak forest, while the bluffs support a growth of mature magnolias, beeches and hickories.

Starting down towards the river, the trail passes a series of six depressions that were once Confederate gun pits guarding the river. Some of the pits are still connected by a system of trenches.

Apparently the river was the expected path of a northern force wishing to capture the valuable cotton stores in Apalachicola. But when

76

the Union forces did come to Apalachicola it was from the Gulf of Mexico. The guns on the river bluff were never trained on an enemy boat. The troops stationed there eventually saw action in the Battle of Olustee. Ironically, the pits dug for war are today considered prime wildflower viewing areas, especially in the spring.

The trail drops down towards the river through a series of step-like ancient bluffs that mark the river's progress as it cut its way to the bedrock over the eons.

At the river's edge, you can see the current-effects of erosion working away at the bank. The flood plain is characterized by plants like water hickory, sweetgum, overcup oak, and American ash. Bald cypress, tupelo, and Virginia willow thrive in occasional swampy areas with standing water.

The bluffs trail eventually turns away from the river and into a ravine. After passing a small spring, appropriately named Blue Springs, the trail begins a climb back to the Gregory House.

Directions

To reach Torreya State Park from Tallahassee, take Highway 20 west about 3 1/2 miles past Hosford, where you take County Road 271 north into the park. Or take I-10 west to the State Highway 12 Exit. Follow Highway 12 through Greensboro to where it intersects County Road 271 about 10 miles to the west. In both cases, there are Torreya State Park signs marking the turn onto County Road 271.

For further information, write or phone, Torreya State Park, Rt. 2, Box 70, Bristol, FL 32321; (904) 643-2674.

Sandy roads throughout the forest make the wilderness easily accessible.

Apalachicola National Forest
Camping, hiking, biking, canoeing, and wildlife watching

We once heard an employee of the National Forest Service refer to a newly established Munson Hill Off-Road Bike Trail as "an opportunity to invite the public into the forest." He made us realize that public land is only that if the public uses it. And too often the national forest is left only for those that hunt and fish, or harvest trees or honey.

However, visitors to the 560,000-acre Apalachicola National Forest can also go hiking, swimming, bird watching, picnicking, horseback riding, or camping; and it's a great place just to take an evening drive. Of course none of these activities absolutely requires a forest as a backdrop but it does add a special dimension to whatever your chosen activity happens to be.

Roads, trails, and flat terrain make this national forest one of the most accessible in the country. The best way to get started though, is to order a map from the U.S. Forest Service to help guide you when you start out to explore.

A number of paved state highways cross the forest in a north-south direction. The main east-west road is the unpaved Forest Highway 13 which crosses the forest between Crawfordville and Wilma. An entire myriad of dirt roads criss-cross the forest between the highways. The eastern section of Highway 13 between Crawfordville and the Ochlockonee River is passable by cars. From the Ochlockonee River west, the road is soft in places and requires a four-wheel drive vehicle or at least a truck with high clearance.

Highway 13 will give you a good introduction to the forest. The woods along the road alternate between uplands and wetlands. The former is largely covered with various species of pines towering over a diverse understory. The wetlands are thick with titi, bald cypress, Virginia willows, black gums, bays and red maples.

Wildflowers and Wildlife

Wildflowers and understory plants bloom at different times of the year providing an ever-changing scenery. Wildflowers common along the roads include; meadow beauty, golden coreopsis, hatpin, wax myrtle, marsh pin, yellow-eyed grass, button bush, and wild azalea.

Spotting wildlife can be a little more difficult, but you can increase your chances with the proper timing. Sunrise and sunset are when many mammals and birds are on the move. But if that's inconvenient, or you prefer not to share the time with the mosquitoes, try a cool, cloudy day. Squirrels, rabbits, deer, otter, turkey and bobcat can all be seen crossing the roads from time to time.

Stop in the middle of a mature pineland and you might hear the unmistakable pounding of a pileated woodpecker, or witness the undulating flight of a red-headed woodpecker.

Other birds common to the forest include brown thrashers, eastern kingbirds, and flycatchers. Sometimes a barred owl can be spotted on a high tree branch, or a hawk circling high overhead can be glimpsed through a gap in the trees.

Take time to walk along the dirt roads looking for animal tracks. A track identification book can add a new dimension to a forest visit. You'll be quickly reminded of whose home it really is.

Biking and Hiking

If you want to give up the engine but not the wheels, you can ride off-road bicycles on any of the dirt roads or try the Munson Hills Off-Road Bicycle Trail. The trail begins and ends about 1.25 miles south of the trailhead of the Tallahassee-St. Marks Historic Railroad State Trail. A sign posted above the St. Marks Trail marks the turn onto the Munson Hills Trail and into the national forest. (See page 50.)

If you care to abandon wheels completely, you can stroll for an hour or a month on hiking trails and roads in the forest. In addition, a 67-mile section of the Florida National Scenic Trail crosses the forest passing through live oak and cabbage palm hammocks, mature pine forests, and wet, dark swamps. It looks out over sink holes and salt marsh vistas; and it follows winding, wilderness rivers, crosses sandy-bottomed creeks, and sneaks past hidden, forested lakes. (See page 9.)

Perhaps the most impressive section of the Florida Trail is a 15-mile

Hidden lakes scattered through the forest are easily accessible with a canoe.

stretch through the 25,600-acre, federally-designated, Bradwell Bay Wilderness Area, which is named for a man who spent a number of days lost in the swamp.

A walk through Bradwell Bay means snakes, alligators, mud and mosquitoes. But it can also mean towering, moss-laden cypress trees, jungle-like vegetation, wildlife, and a chance to make contact with nature that just doesn't present itself in tamer outdoor pursuits. (For an expanded description of Bradwell Bay see page 17.)

Another part of the Florida Scenic Trail passes through the Leon Sinks Geological Area which is located six miles south of Tallahassee on Highway 319. The area sports numerous large sink holes, a cave and a creek that disappears underground. (For more information on Leon Sinks see page 21.)

Canoeing and Kayaking

If you want to get entirely off your feet, you can take advantage of canoe and kayaking opportunities in Lost Creek, Bradford Brook, the Ochlockonee River and many of the streams connecting to the Apalachicola.

All of these waterways fluctuate according to current rainfall conditions and except for the Ochlockonee River, may be impassable during low water. Numerous recreation areas and landings along the Ochlockonee provide access for short trips along the 60 miles of river.

Also, all of the lakes and ponds in the forest are open to paddlers wishing to explore a cypress-covered shoreline, or paddle across a quiet lake looking for turtles and alligators while absorbing the stress-relief scenery.

Pictured above is a nesting cavity of the red-cockaded woodpecker. The largest population in the world of this endangered species resides in the Apalachicola National Forest.

Trout Pond-Disabled Access Recreation Area

Located about five miles south of Capital Circle on Spring Hill Road, Trout Pond is a recreation area designed with access for the disabled. There's a paved nature trail around the lake, plus accessible picnic areas and a fishing pier.

The Forest Service is also in the process of installing a swimming pool adapted for disabled use.

Recreation Areas—Camping

There are also a number of Forest Service-maintained recreation areas throughout the forest. Many offer picnicking, camping, and swimming opportunities. Silver Lake and Lost Lake are popular areas near Tallahassee.

If you want to strike out on your own, there are plenty of trails and roads to choose from. Plan your own trip and find your own special places. Camping is permitted anywhere in the forest, except during hunting season when it is restricted to certain designated recreation areas. Anytime you plan to wander off into the woods, take precautions against chiggers, ticks, and mosquitos; always carry a compass and a map; and take plenty of water.

Fishing

All of the forest lakes and rivers are open to fishing under the jurisdiction and rules of the Florida Game and Fresh Water Fish Commission. Most of the lakes offer moderately good bream and largemouth bass fishing. A reliable approach for both is to paddle along offshore while casting a small spinner towards the shoreline vegetation.

> **The forest is divided into two districts. Contact the U.S. Forest Service in either district office for information on current trail and road conditions, and water levels. Apalachicola District: State Road 20, P.O. Box 579, Bristol, FL 32321, (904) 643-2282; Wakulla District: U.S. Highway 319, Route 6, Box 7860, Crawfordville, FL 32327, (904) 926-3561.**
>
> **To order a map of the Apalachicola National Forest, send $2 per map to the U.S. Forest Service, 325 John Knox Road, Suite F-100, Tallahassee, FL 32303.**

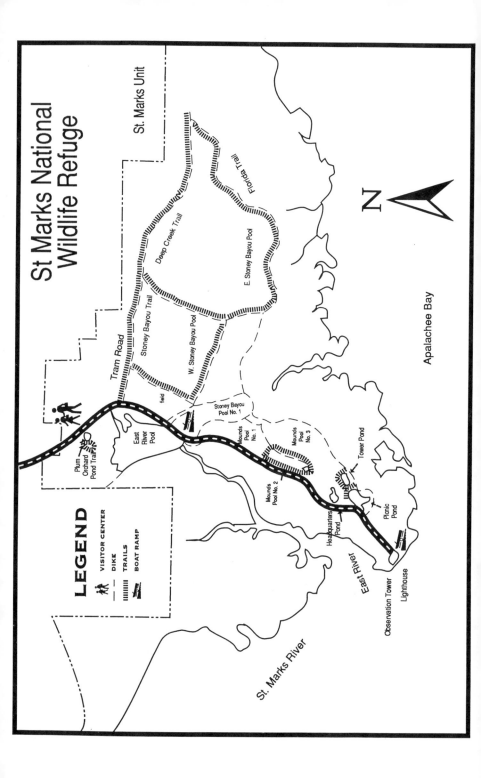

St. Marks National Wildlife Refuge

Focus on wildlife and lots more

We all know Florida is a tourist state, but not just for people. Every year thousands and thousands of birds also choose to winter in the St. Marks National Wildlife Refuge about 20 miles south of Tallahassee on the Gulf Coast. In addition, thousands more stop by on their way to more exotic lands of the Bahamas and South America.

About 31,000 acres of Apalachee Bay and 64,000 acres of saltmarsh, freshwater marsh, hardwood swamps, pine woods and impoundments provide a vacation land, rest stop, or permanent home for 272 species of birds from North America. Although birds use the refuge year-round it's during the winter that populations swell to impressive numbers.

Nevertheless, you can hardly visit the refuge any time of the year without seeing something new: a family of raccoons, a colorful snake, a deer, an alligator or a new roadside wildflower in bloom that you missed last time.

Actually, the original purpose of the refuge when it was created in the 1930s was to enhance migratory waterfowl populations by providing an inviting habitat that included a bountiful food supply. At that time dikes were built by the Civilian Conservation Corps, creating expansive pools in which salinity could be controlled. Different salinities allow for growth of distinct vegetation preferred by different waterfowl species. In the 1970s the large impoundments were subdivided by cross dikes in order to increase management capabilities.

However, if you're a beginning or experienced birder the first place to stop is always the visitor center. Talk to the personnel on duty - ask them about any unusual recent sightings. If you're new to the refuge have them suggest a couple good spots that have been active lately, or they might suggest a hike that will give you a variety of opportunities.

Also check the wildlife sightings book that is kept on the information counter. Previous visitors will have jotted down interesting or unusual wildlife they had seen, and if it was recent enough you might have the same luck. Don't forget to add your sightings to the book on the way out.

If you don't already have one, pick up a bird identification book at the visitor center along with a pamphlet titled the Birds of St. Marks. Also, ask for a map of the pools and the dikes. Ducks at a Distance, a booklet published by the Game and Fresh Water Fish Commission, explains how to identify ducks from afar by recognizing size, shape, flocking behavior, voice and habitat choices. Finally, no birdwatching venture is complete without a pair of binoculars - colors and distinctive markings are hard to see without them.

One way to get started is to ride past the pools and forest all the way to the lighthouse on the Gulf; pulling off for a closer look anytime you see something of interest. Then work your way back toward the main entrance stopping to scan impoundments or take one of the nature trails or dike hikes.

Any time you're in the refuge watch the skies and trees for circling or perching hawks, osprey, falcons, and bald eagles. There are numerous pairs of bald eagles nesting in the refuge every year. Ask directions at the visitor center if you want to view an eagle's nest. And watch the wires along the road for perching birds like swallows, mocking birds, and eastern kingbirds.

At the end of the road, look for rafts of bay ducks out on Apalachee Bay in the winter, you might see redheads, scalps, and hooded mergansers from shore. These species are also called diving ducks because of the ability to dive up to 10 feet underwater looking for fish, shellfish and underwater vegetation.

The saltmarsh around the lighthouse is usually dotted with a variety of wading birds like great blue herons, white ibis, glossy ibis, little blue herons and maybe a reddish egret. This is also a good place to see clapper rails and long-billed marsh wrens, and check the wires for an occasional scissortailed flycatcher.

Lighthouse Pool, across the road from the lighthouse has a high salinity and also attracts bay ducks including mallards, shovelers, widgeons, and canvasbacks.

Picnic Pond, a few miles up the road, is easily identifiable by the osprey nest in the lone tree on the opposite shore. Here again the salinity is high enough to attract bay ducks. Look for hooded mergansers,

The refuge belongs to the wildlife and man is only a visitor.

buffleheads, canvasbacks, redheads and ringnecks.

Just above Picnic Pond is the start of the Mounds Pool Interpretive Trail which gives the hiker an opportunity to see birds in different environments. The live oak hammock is a popular rest area for migrating warblers in spring and fall. Late February to early March is a good time to see these birds.

Farther up the road at Headquarters Pond, look for wood storks and blackcrowned night herons. Water here is fairly fresh, so Headquarters Pond attracts a variety of puddle ducks, also called dabbling ducks known for tipping and dabbling at vegetation just beneath the surface.

The best bird-watching in the winter takes place the few days following a strong cold front. It's also a good idea to take the angle of the sun into consideration when choosing which trail to walk, or which pool to scan. For the best viewing you want the sun at your back. Many waterfowl colors are iridescent, especially the dabblers. Direct sunlight makes it easier to see the birds' full colors. For instance, Lighthouse Pool is best for viewing in the early morning. So is Tower Pond, and Mounds No. 3 if you take a trail around to the eastern side.

There are simply hundreds of other bird species both rare and common that can be spotted in the refuge: forster's tern, golden eagle, hooded warbler, eastern kingbird, sandhill crane, yellowlegs, groove-billed ani, great horned owl, common screech owl, Florida gallinule, ruddy duck, and blue grosbeak, to name just a few. But the fun is to find these species yourself.

Hiking and Biking

Fortunately, the 18 miles of dikes surrounding the 11 impoundments also serve as excellent walking or bicycle trails and give the birdwatcher an opportunity to see different species taking advantage of various habitats. The dikes can be walked in a number of combinations of short and long hikes.

The four miles of dikes around Stoney Bayou Pool No. 1 are popular because the hiker can circle the pool back to the main road, then walk along the road back to the car. The dikes around Mounds Pool No. 1 also offer excellent bird viewing opportunities, and a circular hike back to the car.

There are also two designated nature trails in the refuge of eight and twelve miles. They take advantage of primitive roads and impoundment dikes. (See page 53 for more information on bicycling in the refuge.)

Fishing

Fishing is permitted in any of the refuge pools from March 15 to October 15. The pools are closed to boats during the rest of the year to protect the migrating waterfowl.

Boats must be hand powered or have a 10 horsepower or smaller engine. There is a small ramp leading into the East River Pool and another across the road in Stoney Bayou Number 1. Dragging your boat over the dikes from one pool into another is also permitted.

Camping

Camping is permitted in the refuge only at designated campsites along the Florida Trail for overnight trail users. Some other restrictions may apply. A permit must be obtained a full 15 days prior to your trip. However, there is a public campground on U.S. Highway 98 (where it crosses the St. Marks River) at the turnoff onto County Road 59. This campground is often full during hunting season.

Miles off the main road the impoundment dikes offer a wonderful vista of the saltmarsh.

Directions
St. Marks Refuge is in Wakulla County. The main unit is located three miles south of U. S. Highway 98 on County Road 59. To find C.R. 59 on the map look for where the St. Marks River crosses Highway 98.

There is a small fee to enter the refuge, or you can purchase a Federal Duck Stamp at the Visitor Center which is good for one year. The Visitor Center is open 8 a.m. to 4:15 p.m. Monday through Friday and 10 a.m. to 5 p.m. on weekends. For more information contact St. Marks National Wildlife Refuge, P.O. Box 68, St. Marks, 32355; (904) 925-6121.

Information Resources

State and National Parks

Apalachicola National Estuarine Research Reserve (ANERR): 261 - 7th Street, Apalachicola FL 32320; (904) 653-8063.

Florida Caverns State Park: 2701 Caverns Road, Marianna, FL 32446; (904) 482-9598.

St. George Island State Park: P.O. Box 62, Eastpoint, FL 32328; (904) 927-2111 or (904) 670-2111.

St. Joseph Peninsula State Park: Star Route 1, Box 200, Port St. Joe, FL 32456; (904) 227-1327.

St. Marks National Wildlife Refuge: P.O. Box 68, St. Marks, FL 32355; (904) 925-6121.

Torreya State Park: Rt. 2, Box 70, Bristol, FL 32321; (904) 643-2674.

Wakulla Springs State Park: Wakulla Springs Road, Wakulla Springs, FL 32305; (904) 922-3632 for information on boat tours and nature trails; or (904) 224-5950 for accommodations.

State and National Governmental Agencies

U.S. Forest Service: 325 John Knox Road, Suite F-100, Tallahassee, FL 32303; (904) 942-9300. Maps of the Apalachicola National Forest can be obtained by sending $2.00 to this address.

Apalachicola District: State Road 20, P.O. Box 579, Bristol, FL 32321; (904) 643-2282.

Wakulla District: U.S. Highway 319, Route 6, Box 7860, Crawfordville, FL 32327, (904) 926-3561.

Department of Environmental Protection: Division of Recreation and Parks, Office of Public Relations, 3900 Commonwealth Boulevard, M.S. #535, Tallahassee, FL 32399; (904) 488-9872.

State and Local Recreational Organizations

Florida Trail Association: P.O. Box 13708, Gainesville, FL 32604-1708; 1(800) 343-1882 or 1(904) 378-8823.

Capital City Cyclists: P.O. Box 4222, Tallahassee, FL 32315-4222.

Cyclelogical: 4780 Woodville Highway, Tallahassee, FL 32311; (904) 656-0001.

Apalachee Canoe Club: P.O. Box 4027, Tallahassee, FL 32315.

Canoe Rentals

The Canoe Shop: 1115 W. Orange Avenue, Tallahassee, FL 32310, (904) 576-5335. Ask for Sam Lamar.

TNT Hideaway: Highway 98, St. Marks, FL 32355; (904) 925-6412.

Other Books Available from Woodland Productions

To order additional copies of *Florida's Outdoors*, or one of the Fishing the Big Bend series please use the order form above.